Part of the John A. Moreels MBE photo archive.

- THIRD SELECTION OF WORK -

*Featuring over a century of photographs,
views, etchings and engravings.*

*The North of England as seen by a family
of photographers who were founders in
the development of photographic art.*

compiled by
John A. Moreels MBE
'Photo Memories Organisation'

*Best wishes
John*

LOTTERY FUNDED

Photo Memories Organisation,
Durham City. DH1 5XD. U.K.
www.photomemoriesarchive.org.uk

First Published 2014

Publishing and Copyright 2014 by:
Photo Memories Organisation
Durham City. DH1 5XD. U.K.

www.photomemoriesarchive.org.uk

Printed By:
Potts Print (UK)
Atlas House
Nelson Park
Cramlington
Northumberland
NE23 1WG

I.S.B.N. 978-0-9534224-5-6

Introduction

The third selection of work – another picture book.

It is now 16 years (1998) since the first selection of 'Nostalgic Views of the North' was published with the second selection being produced the following year (1999). Doesn't time go fast? The comments and support we received relating to the collection which was restored over 6 years ago, gave us the incentive to try and restore more of the collection. Thanks to the support of the Heritage Lottery Fund in 2013, our group of dedicated volunteers have scanned, restored and researched many more exciting images. We are delighted to be able to share some of these in this new book.

We have now digitised and identified approximately 15% of the full collection which continues to enthral us with the vast array of images of the North of England. The brilliant talents of the artists, engravers and photographers have captured unique images which take us back in time to love and appreciate life in the region for the past 300 years.

The photographs always produce many more questions while providing answers with their pictorial images. Every day we are privileged to learn more facts about the region and we never imagined that the same enthusiasm and excitement for sharing nostalgic knowledge and memories would be forthcoming from so many of you. Thank you, your compliments and comments are warmly appreciated:-

'you have discovered a most interesting treasure of historic photographs, with much more work still to be done.'	S.J. Newcastle.
'The members certainly enjoyed seeing the etchings and photographs and the details which you gave us'	M.R. Cullercoats.
'some members well into their 90's – reliving some of their earliest days as they watched the images'	L.N. Haydon Br.
'What a collection and what an achievement to produce the pictures into a wonderful book'	J.E. Gosforth
'fascinated by your discovery of that unbelievable glass plate collection'	R.M. Cleveland.
'members have been full of praise for the content, quality and style'	R.H. Newcastle.
'Extremely interesting'	V.R. Consett.

Many thanks to the numerous contributions from people which have helped in the updating of the previous two books and with notes and observations to enhance the brief notes and facts accompanying the photographs in this third book. We are aware that many publications and editorials have been utilised by these people and unfortunately too many for us to list or even be aware of for their inclusion. We also believe that the facts provided to us have been researched and are factually correct, but we cannot be certain or guarantee them. Our great appreciation goes to the researchers and contributors and to the fantastic array of local and national material which have provided the interesting comments. We would urge all of you to regard our books as picture books and use the images to obtain more knowledge and information relating to the specific scene or historic view. We hope we can help jog your memory with our images and motivate you to investigate your local history and nostalgia. Together we can share those interesting historical memories and facts which can be shared with generations to come.

Our website – **www.photomemoriesarchive.org.uk** - features many images and is constantly updated as and when we discover more interesting photographs to save and share. We need your help, your memories, your knowledge and any interesting facts relating to the images. Please visit our website to share your information and help us research these fascinating images by adding your comments.

Thank you and best wishes from all of us at **'Photo Memories Organisation'**.

John A. Moreels MBE

heritage lottery fund
LOTTERY FUNDED

This book features a small selection of images from the collection produced by the masters of engraving, etching and photography…

Ref 3000.

Ref 3001.

Ref 3002.

Cushie Butterfield

This popular song in the mining communities of the North East is now a famous local piece which pokes fun at Cushie, a whitening stone seller. The stone, made of baked clay (called yellow clay) was used to clean and decorate the stone steps leading up to the front door of the many terraced houses in the area. It is also believed that pitmen used the 'yeller clay' to make candlesticks. Geordie Ridley had to leave the area for a while when the song caused anger with Cushie's relatives.
It appears to be the last song written by Ridley who died when only 30 years old.

Ref 3162a

A traditional folk song written by Geordie Ridley (1835–1864) and first published in 1862 by Thomas Allan. Sung to the tune of the music hall song "Pretty Polly Perkins."

Ah's a broken-hearted keelman, an' aw's owerheed in luv,
Wiv a yung lass in Gyetshead, an' aw calls her me duv,
Her nyem's Cushy Butterfield, an' she sells yeller clay,
An' her cusin is a muckman, an' they call him Tom Gray.

> *Chorus:*
> *She's a big lass, an' a bonny lass,*
> *An' she likes her beer;*
> *An' they call her Cushy Butterfield,*
> *An' aw wish she was here.*

Her eyes are like two holes in a blanket burnt throo,
An' her brows in a morning wad spyen a yung coo;
An' when aw hear her shootin " Will ye buy ony clay,"
Like a candy man's trumpet, it steals maw young heart away.

> *Chorus:*
> *She's a big lass, an' a bonny lass,*
> *An' she likes her beer;*
> *An' they call her Cushy Butterfield,*
> *An' aw wish she was here.*

Ye'll oft see hor doon at Sandgate when the fresh herrrin cums in;
She's like a bagful o'sawdust tied roond wiv a string;
She weers big golashes, te, an' her stockins was once white,
An' her bedgoon is a lelock, an' her hat's nivor strite.

> *Chorus:*
> *She's a big lass, an' a bonny lass,*
> *An' she likes her beer;*
> *An' they call her Cushy Butterfield,*
> *An' aw wish she was here.*

When aw axed her te marry me, she started te laff,
"Noo, nyen o' yor munkey tricks, for aw like ne such chaff!"
Then she start'd a bubblin, an' she roar'd like a bull,
An' the cheps i' the keel says aw'm nowt but a fyeul.

> *Chorus:*
> *She's a big lass, an' a bonny lass,*
> *An' she likes her beer;*
> *An' they call her Cushy Butterfield,*
> *An' aw wish she was here.*

She says, "The chep that gets me'll heh te work ivry day,
An' when he cums hyem at neets he'll heh te gan an' seek clay,
An' when he's away seekin't aw'll myek balls an' sing,
Weel may the keel row that maw laddie's in!

> *Chorus:*
> *She's a big lass, an' a bonny lass,*
> *An' she likes her beer;*
> *An' they call her Cushy Butterfield,*
> *An' aw wish she was here.*

Durham Cathedral is a masterpiece of Romanesque (or Norman) architecture. It was begun in 1093 and largely completed within 40 years. It is the only cathedral in England to retain almost all of its Norman craftsmanship and one of a few to preserve the unity and integrity of its original design. The castle and cathedral are built on a peninsula of land created by a loop in the River Wear which is crossed on the east side of the city by the Elvet Bridge. A grade 1 listed medieval masonry arch bridge built in 1160 by Bishop Pudsey (1153 – 1195). *Ref 3008.*

Old map of Northumberland (NORTHVMBRIAE)
Ref map 0001.

Old map of County Durham (DVNELMENSIS)
Ref map 0002.

Hartlepool from Streaton Sands. Hartlepool was founded in the 7th century around Hartlepool Abbey. It grew in the Middle Ages developing a harbour which was then the official port of County Durham. *Ref 3009.*

An engraving of Stockton on Tees High Street from the north. The Town House, in the distance, was built in 1735 with the first theatre opening in 1766. Stockton's market can trace its history to 1310 when Bishop Bek of Durham granted a market charter – *'to our town of Stockton, a market upon every Wednesday for ever'*. The Parish Church of St. Thomas is on the left. *Ref 3010.*

Raby Castle. A medieval castle built in the 14th century by John Neville. The castle is situated in a 200 acre deer park. *Ref 3011.*

Ref 3012. Great Bridge of Tyne – It was built in 1260 and then washed away in the great floods of 16th/17th November 1771. Part was washed away in the 1339 flood and rebuilt. Two thirds of the way across the bridge from Newcastle were two blue marble stones, called St. Cuthbert's Stones, which marked the boundary between the jurisdiction of Newcastle Corporation and the Bishop of Durham.

Great Bridge of Tyne with a view of the Quayside, Newcastle upon Tyne and the city walls. Looking north, you can see St. Nicholas Cathedral and the Castle Keep in the centre. *Ref 3013.*

St. Nicholas Cathedral. The earliest fragments date from 1175. Most of the Cathedral dates from 14th & 15th century. It was used as a navigation point for ships on the river for over 500 years. *Ref 3014.*

Central Station, Newcastle upon Tyne. – built in 1849. Designed by John Dobson for the York, Newcastle & Berwick Railway Company and opened on the 29th August 1850 by Queen Victoria as was the Hotel. The portico was designed by Thomas Prosser and added to the station entrance in 1863. *Ref 3015.*

Bottom of Dean Street, Newcastle upon Tyne. The street was formed, in 1869, over a dene (burn) which flows into the River Tyne. The Lort Burn had been an open sewer. It was originally called Dene Street. *Ref 3016.*

Head of 'the Side' and Admiral Collingwood's Birthplace, Newcastle upon Tyne. Collingwood was born on the 26th September 1748. This is one of Newcastle's remaining medieval streets. *Ref 3017.*

Castle Keep and Court House. The Castle Keep pre-dated the city walls. It is a Grade 1 listed building built by Robert Curthose, son of William the Conqueror, in 1080. It was later rebuilt by Maurice the Engineer for Henry II between (1168 - 1178) *Ref 3018.*

Grainger Street, Newcastle upon Tyne. Designed in the 1830's by Richard Grainger. 40% of the buildings are now listed. Grey's Monument erected 1838 commemorating the role of Prime Minister Charles Grey, 2nd Earl Grey, in the passing of the Reform Act in 1832. *Ref 3019.*

Birth place of Mark Akenside, (1721-1770) English poet & physician, son of a butcher who lived at Butcher Bank, Newcastle upon Tyne. *Ref 3020.*

The Black Gate, Newcastle upon Tyne.
Built between 1247 and 1250 during the
reign of Henry III and the last addition
to the medieval castle defences.
The arched passageway, with guard chambers
on either side of the gatehouse of the barbican,
was a walled defensive entrance for the castle's
North Gate. *Ref 3021.*

Chillingham Park and Castle, Northumberland. A medieval castle owned by the family of the Earls Grey since the 12th century. It was originally a monastery. *Ref 3022.*

Alnwick Castle, Northumberland, was originally owned by the Vescy family with the first parts being erected in about 1096. When the Vescy family became extinct Alnwick Castle and the surrounding manor were bequeathed to Antony Bek the Bishop of Durham. The Percy family benefited from England's wars with Scotland and through the military accomplishments by Henry Percy, 1st Baron Percy (1273-1314), enhanced his family status in northern England. In 1309 Henry Percy purchased the barony of Alnwick from Antony Bek, and Alnwick Castle has been owned by the Percy family (Dukes of Northumberland) ever since. In 1345 the Percy family also acquired Warkworth Castle. *Ref 3023.*

Lambton Hall (Castle), Chester le Street, Durham. The ancestral seat of the Lambton family, the Earls of Durham. Originally a 17th century mansion named Harraton Hall. Lambton Castle was constructed in its present form in the early 19th century by John George Lambton, first Earl of Durham and one time Governor General of Canada. Designed in the style of a Norman castle by architects Joseph Bonomi the Elder and his son Ignatius, it overlooks the wooded Wear Valley and was funded with coal mining wealth accumulated from the mines which ran underneath the castle grounds. *Ref 3024.*

Royal Grammar School R.G.S. Westgate Road site, Newcastle upon Tyne (1810) R.G.S. was founded in 1525 by Thomas Horsley within the grounds of St. Nicholas Church. The site has moved five times since then, most recently in 1906 to Jesmond. *Ref 3025. Cat C3973.*

Market Place, Morpeth. Situated on the River Wansbeck. It was given permission to hold a market in 1199 and by the mid-18th century had one of the most important cattle markets in the country. *Ref 3026.*

Brinkburn Priory. Medieval monastery on the bend of the River Coquet, approx. 4 miles east of Rothbury, Northumberland. *Ref 3027.*

Warkworth Castle. An early 12th century motte & bailey castle. Captured by the Scots in 1644 & 1645 and used as a prison in the 16th century. *Ref 3028.*

Bamburgh Castle. Ida, the Saxon monarch and founder of the dynasty of Northumbria Kings, first built the castle in 547. The settlement was named 'Bebbanburgh' after Bebba, the wife of Ida's grandson. In 993, the Vikings destroyed the original fortification. The Normans built a new castle on the site which was completed by Henry II around 1095. Note the windmill. The blades were removed from the windmill in the 1700's but the base still remains. *Ref 3029.*

Bywell Bay, Northumberland. Painted by William Bellers (1749-1773). Etched & Engraved by Messrs'. Mason & Canot. *Ref 3030.*

Cullercoats Bay, sitting between Tynemouth and Whitley Bay. A semi-circular sandy beach with cliffs and caves. Historically, the village port was used to export both salt and coal, but the railways relocated coal shipments to better harbours. Fishing then became the main industry. *Ref 3031.*

Clifford's Fort, North Shields. Built in 1672 at the beginning of the Dutch War to protect the mouth of the River Tyne and prevent warships from entering the river. Designed by Swedish military engineer Martin Beckman and built by a Yorkshire architect, Robert Trollope. It also played a part in the Napoleonic wars and by 1677 the fort mounted up to forty guns. Circa 1788. *Ref 3032.*

North Shields from the high ground north east of the Low Light erected in the early 16th century by the Master and Brethren of Trinity House. The High Light was built in 1808 replacing the Old High Beacon built in 1727. The Low Light at the eastern end of Low Street operated in conjunction with the High Light to guide vessels into the safe channel of the River Tyne. Engraving from drawing by J.W. Carmichael. (1800-1868). *Ref 3033.*

North Shields near the Wooden Bridge, looking east. Until the opening of the New Quay the stretch of foreshore east and west of the Wooden Bridge was the principle terminus of river traffic. Engraving from drawing by J.W. Carmichael. (1800-1868) Circa.1830 *Ref 3034.*

The Tyne at North Shields. The High lights and Low lights are behind the Fish Quay. *Ref 3035.*

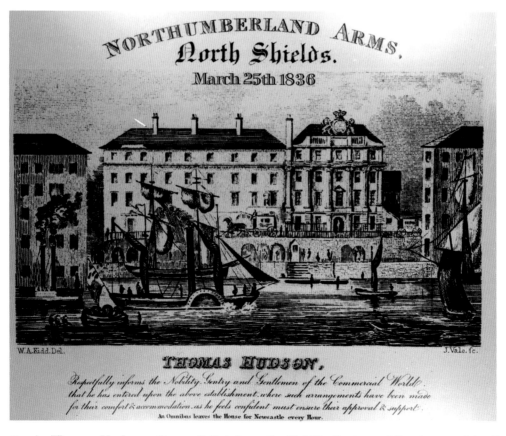

An Invitation to attend…**Thomas Hudson** – Respectfully informs the Nobility, Gentry and Gentlemen of the Commercial World that he has entered upon the above establishment where such arrangements have been made for their comfort & accommodation, as he feels confident must ensure their approval & support. An Omnibus leaves the House for Newcastle every hour. *Ref 3036.*

Vaux Brewery at the Newcastle Jubilee Exhibition in 1887. Vaux Brewery was founded in 1837, in Sunderland, by Cuthbert Vaux (1813 – 1878), the son of Cuthbert Vaux senior, a master mariner. One of the first British brewers to introduce bottled ales and stouts. The brewery closed on the 2nd July 1999. *Ref 3037.*

A Christmas present from Vaux… Don't forget to collect your free pen when you buy two bottles of Double Maxim. The pen contains enough ink to draw a line over 2 miles long! *Ref 3038.*

A COLLECTION OF NORTH EAST BEER ADVERTS & LOGOS.

Federation Brewery Rocket Ale. *Ref 3039.*

Newcastle Breweries Beers. *Ref 3040.*

Federation Brewery High Level Brown Ale. *Ref 3041.*

The first business premises in Cuthbert Street of the
Blaydon Co-operative Society. It opened in 1858 with
only 38 members.
It was the second Co-operative Union in the country.
Rochdale being the first to open a shop on the 21st
December 1844.
Co-operative Societies operated for the benefit of its
customers, known as members. Members had shares
and received annual dividends based on their
purchases. *Ref 3042.*

The Co-operative grows from a house to
a street. A distinctive store building on
Church Street shows how quickly the
Blaydon Co-operative Society grew and
expanded into much larger premises.
Ref 3043.

A typical interior of a Co-operative
store. Owned by the members and
operated by a members committee.
The idea of co-operative trading
revolutionised food retailing with
dividend, often known as 'divi' and
the 'divi number' became a part of
British Life. *Ref 3044.*

Make a FRESH start...

Moving into a new house?... then be sure to ask for an *electric* cooker. Electricity is *clean*, kind to your kitchen furnishings and curtains, and an electric cooker's positive control makes perfect cooking easier still.

Then electricity itself is so cheap — on the '1d. Economy Plan' a full day's cooking for a family of four costs only about 4d.

...with an **ELECTRIC Cooker**

Ask for your copy of the '1d. Economy Plan' leaflet – it tells you how to save with electricity

ELECTRICITY SERVICE CENTRE
THE NORTH EASTERN ELECTRICITY BOARD
CARLIOL HOUSE, NEWCASTLE UPON TYNE

M30/50

Electric Ovens began to compete with Gas Ovens in late 1920s/early 1930s, although they were available as early as the 1890's. *Ref 3046.*

Fancy a new motorised vehicle? A car, scooter or motorbike, or a hoovermatic for the wife! Check out these adverts from the 1950-1960's.

Murphy Radio was founded in 1929 in Welwyn Garden City by Frank Murphy and E.J. Power as a volume manufacturer of home and armed forces radio sets. *Ref 3048.*

No other running expenses whatever happens

RENT murphy

the latest 17"
murphy
£4 DOWN
and
PER 10/6 WEEK

R. CARRUTHERS & SON
LOW FELL AND FELLING
FOR RENTAL SERVICE.

at **COWIES**
£359·19·6
EASIEST H.P.TERMS
Plus Model **ISETTA**

BMW Isetta Bubble Car launched April 1962. Built in Brighton. *Ref 3045.*

£159·10·7
TRIUMPH *Tigress* SCOOTER
£33 DEPOSIT
36 MONTHLY PAYMENTS OF
£4·14·2

Triumph Tigress scooter also known as BSA Sunbeam built 1959 – 1964. *Ref 3047.*

BSA 350 OHV STAR MODEL B40
£205
OR ONLY
£42 Deposit
AND 36 MONTHLY PAYMENTS OF
£6-1-0

BSA announces B40 Star in 1960 as a replacement Dispatch Rider machine for the British Army and designed to the armies specifications. *Ref 3049.*

see the amazing **HOOVERMATIC**

Hoover Electric Washing Machines were established in Merthyr Tydfil, Wales on the 19th Oct 1948, and closed on the 13th March 2009. Hoovermatic Twin Tub was launched in 1957. *Ref 3050.*

Shopping at Binns

Best of branded goods. Unhurried choice—your leisure is Binns pleasure.

Efficient service. Fast moving stock—ensuring new ideas, fresh stock. Value *plus*. Come often to Binns. Look around, or enjoy down-to-earth shopping. Relax there with morning coffee or later meal. Bring the children too. Treat them to summertime drinks. To stroll round Binns is to see the latest and loveliest for home and family.

GO SHOPPING AT BINNS

From a drapery shop to the largest department store in Sunderland. Founded by George & Henry Binns in 1807. Acquired by House of Fraser in 1953. *Ref 3052.*

ISAAC WALTON'S *understand* School Outfitting. "Yer canna whack 'em."

'Yer canna whack 'em', in Newcastle since 1887, Isaac Walton & Co. The outfitter to service a man from school to his last day at work. You can still buy starched collars from them at their shop in Newcastle. *Ref 3051.*

Famous Brands... with North East connections.

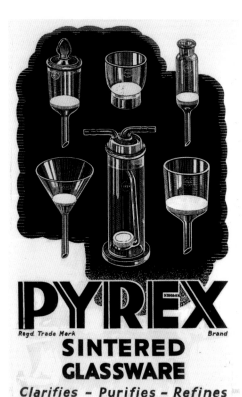

PYREX
Regd. Trade Mark   Brand
SINTERED GLASSWARE
Clarifies – Purifies – Refines

Pyrex was founded in 1915. A brand introduced by Corning of Sunderland and incorporated as a line of clear, low thermal-expansion borosilicate glass used for laboratory glassware and kitchenware. Borosilicate glass was first made by German chemist Otto Schott in 1893. *Ref 3053.*

Stergene
SCIENCE IN CLEANSING

WASHES
WINTER WOOLLIES
WONDERFULLY

Wrights biscuits were established in 1790 by L. Wright & Son, Holborn, South Shields. After a fire in 1898 new buildings were built in Tyne Dock. *Ref 3054.*

Mischief!

Stergene invented by William Handley, an industrial chemist who also produced Domestos in 1929, which was sold door-to-door by salesmen who refilled customers own stoneware jars. It was first produced in a Byker workshop. *Ref 3055.*

Andrews Liver Salt dates back to 1894 when provision importer William Henry Scott and William Murdoch Turner decided there was a future for their health tonic. W.H.Scott & Co. originally based in White Hart Yard. 16, Cloth Market Newcastle moved to 4, Gallowgate, Newcastle in 1891/2 close to St Andrew's Church in Newgate Street.

The product and the building was named 'Andrews' after the church. The trademark was registered in 1909. DIMP insect repellent was also a product of Scott & Turner. *Ref 3056.*

Ref 3057.

North East tea experts Ringtons, founded in 1907, remains a family business and has always retained a sense of its history in all its package designs. The company continues to use old original photographs and the Ringtons' crest in their promotional material. The Ringtons' famous horse and cart has undergone changes with updated designs but has never lost its original image. *Ref 3058.*

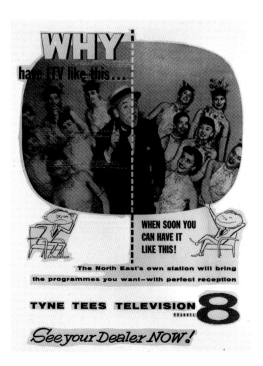

Tyne Tees Television started transmissions on the 15th January 1959 at 5.00 pm. from a converted warehouse in City Road, Newcastle. It was officially opened by the Duke of Northumberland. *Ref 3059.*

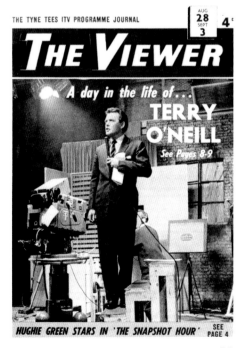

Ref 3060.

At Work in the North East...

If the weather is too wet, the cut hay may spoil in the field before it can be bailed, so there is always intense activity as the hay farmers gather in the hay before it is too late. *Ref 3061.*

Weaving of baskets is as old as the history of man. Baskets were needed as containers for everything imaginable – food, clothing, seeds, storage and transport. Northumbria's fishwives used the 'Back Creel' baskets extensively when carrying fresh fish. *Ref 3062.*

In 1858 Samuel Cotton, a skilled brush maker, was sent to Sunderland by his uncle who owned a brush factory in Hull. The Cotton Brush was started in the Hendon area of Sunderland, supplying coal mines and shipyards. In the centre of the picture is a pitch pan for melting the hot black pitch used as a setting agent to retain the brush filling material in the wood head. *Ref 3063.*

Ladies Sock Making – In 1589 sock making was speeded up by the invention of a loom by William Lee. It was six times faster than hand knitting. In the early 1900's the first circular knitting frames were introduced allowing mass production of socks. *Ref 3064.*

Sack Race, or gunny sack race, is a competitive game where participants place both of their legs inside a sack or pillow case that reaches their waist or neck and jump forward from a starting point toward a finish line. *Ref 3066.*

Greasy pole refers to the pole that has been made slippery and thus difficult to grip. The object is for one person to knock the other participant off the pole with the use of a pillow. The one who stays on the pole is the winner. *Ref 3068.*

A new use for car tyres in the obstacle race. Adults and children enjoy an obstacle race during their sports day. No sign of health and safety in those days. *Ref 3070.*

Egg and spoon race, a sports day event when participants must balance an egg on a spoon and race with it to the finishing line. *Ref 3065.*

A favourite at community events/sports day – three-legged race- is a game of co-operation between partners as much as it is one of speed. It involves two participants attempting to complete a short sprint with the left leg of one runner strapped to the right leg of another runner. The object is for the partners to run together without falling over, and beat the other contestants to the finish line. *Ref 3067.*

Tug of War also known as tug o' war, rope pulling, rope war is a sport that directly pits two teams against each other in a task of strength. Usually a team of 8 but at the local social event the numbers were regularly exceeded. *Ref 3069.*

A new television in the sitting room. It appears you even needed a box to lift it up to a suitable viewing level. *Ref 3072.*

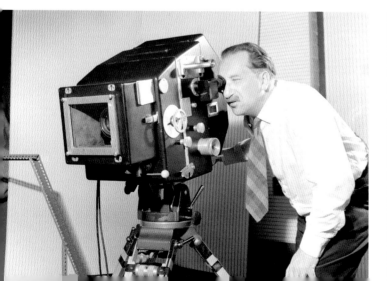

The first British television broadcast was made by Baird Television's electromechanical system over the BBC radio transmitter in September 1929. Baird provided a limited amount of programming five days a week by 1930.

Don't forget to check it is working before it is returned to the customer. *Ref 3074.*

A television studio camera was not very portable in the 1950s/60s. *Ref 3075.*

Remember the days of New Technology?

This is your Life! - Eamon Andrews C.B.E. (Dec 1922 – Nov 1987) presented the programme from its inception in 1955. Here he seems to be introducing a new 'modern' wooden boxed television. *Ref 3071.*

Televisions regularly broke down, but a local repairer would always fix them in his workshop. *Ref 3073.*

A tape recorder was equally a very bulky item with its large tape reels. *Ref 3076.*

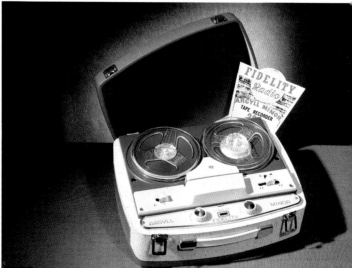

Standing high on a basalt outcrop, overlooking the North Sea, Bamburgh Castle is one of the most impressive looking castles in England. It is visible for many miles, and from its battlements offers views of Lindisfarne Castle on Holy Island, the Farne Islands and the Cheviot Hills. One of the oldest buildings remaining is a large Norman Keep, probably built by Henry II. *Ref 3077.*

Alnwick Castle guards a road crossing the River Aln. Yves de Vescy, Baron of Alnwick, erected the first parts of the castle around 1096. It was built to protect England's northern border against Scottish invasions and border reivers. Alnwick castle was captured in 1136 by King David I of Scotland. It was besieged in 1172 and 1174 by William the Lion, King of Scotland. William was captured outside the walls during the Battle of Alnwick. King John ordered the demolition of Alnwick Castle in 1212 as he considered its existence as a threat from Eustace de Vesci, Lord of Alnwick, but King John's instructions were never carried out. *Ref 3078.*

Cragside in the Parish of Cartington, Northumberland was the first house In the world to be lit by Hydroelectric power. It was built in 1863 on Cragend Hill, a rocky hillside. Originally a modest two-storey lodge and then extended to designs by Norman Shaw, transforming it into an elaborate mansion in the free tudor style. The building once included an astronomical observatory and a scientific laboratory. It was the country home of Lord Armstrong and was acquired by the National Trust in 1977. *Ref 3079.*

Jesmond Dene Watermill. First of many built in the 19th century. The Old Mill was constructed around 1890 and also known as Mabel's Mill. It was occupied by 3 or 4 generations of the Freeman family as a flour mill. In 1862 Lord William George Armstrong acquired the valley and all milling stopped. *Ref 3080.*

Jesmond Dene is a public park in the east end of Newcastle upon Tyne. It occupies the narrow steep sided valley of the Ouseburn. The Armstrong's first laid out the park during the 1860's reflecting a rural setting with woodland, crags, waterfalls and pools. *Ref 3081.*

Ref 3082. The North East Coast Exhibition at Exhibition Park, Newcastle, was opened by H.R.H. Prince of Wales on the 14th May 1929. It was a symbol of the pride and industrial success of the region and an advertisement for local industry and commerce. During 24 weeks 4,373,138 people attended the exhibition and gold watches were given to each one-millionth visitor. The exhibition closed on the 26th October 1929 with a massive firework display. The military museum is the only building which remained after the exhibition.   Night scene *Ref 3083.*

Tees Transporter Bridge is the furthest downstream bridge across the River Tees connecting Middlesbrough, on the south bank to Port Clarence, on the north bank.

The design was first mooted in 1872 when Charles Smith, manager of Hartlepool Iron Works submitted the scheme to avoid affecting river navigation. It was not until 1910 that construction commenced by Sir William Arthur & Co. of Glasgow. The bridge was officially opened on 17th October 1911 by Prince Arthur of Connaught. *Ref 3084.*

Ref 3085.

Ref 3086.

The Tees Newport Bridge, the first large vertical bridge in Britain. It was opened to traffic on 28th February 1934 by the Duke of York. The bridge spans the River Tees a short distance from the Tees Transporter Bridge, linking Middlesbrough with the borough of Stockton on Tees. Designed by Mott, Hay & Anderson and built by local company Dorman Long. Both companies were also responsible for the Tyne Bridge and the Sydney Harbour Bridge.

New Wearmouth Bridge, Sunderland, opened in 1929, with Vaux horse – drawn drays which operated until Vaux closure in 1999. The bridge was officially opened by the Duke of York (later King George VI) on the 31st October 1929. Designed by Mott, Hay & Anderson who also designed many other famous bridges. It was fabricated by Sir William Arrol & Co. in Dalmarwick Ironworks in Glasgow who also built the Forth Rail Bridge and the steel structure for the Tower Bridge in London. *Ref 3087.*

SHIPBUILDING on the TYNE, WEAR and TEES.

Shipbuilding has long been one of the regions important industries. In 1294 a Newcastle shipyard built a galley for the King's fleet and ships were built at Sunderland from at least 1346 and at Stockton from at least 1470. The early ships were built of wood but during the 19th century there was a move towards building ships of iron.

S.S. ANGORA on the stocks. It was built in 1900 by Armstrong, Whitworth & Co Ltd. (1897-1931) at Low Walker for the Imperial Russian Navy as an icebreaker ferry to connect the Trans-Siberian Railway across Lake Baikal. The S.S. Angora made the four hour crossing carrying passengers and goods (not trains) to link the two railheads until the Circum – Baikal Railway was built. *Ref 3088.*

The North East had a strong tradition for producing ships, making the region famous around the world. During the boom years of the early 1900's the shipyards employed thousands of men with a variety of expertise. *Ref 3089.*

Turbine S.Y. ALBION, built in 1905. Men working at the Neptune Yard, Wallsend of Swan, Hunter & Wigham Richardson, (1903-1963) with a variety of occupations including bumpers up, holders down, rivet catchers, welders, ship fitters, foremen and boiler makers. *Ref 3090.*

RMS MAURETANIA. An ocean liner designed by Leonard Peskett and built by Swan Hunter, Wigham Richardson at Wallsend, for the Cunard Steamship Co.Ltd., Liverpool, with the help of a British Government loan to counter German dominance of the Trans-Atlantic passenger service.

When launched on 20th September 1906, it was the largest and fastest ship in the world with a capacity of 2165 passengers. After her 1907 inaugural season she broke records for the fastest crossing of the Atlantic and gained the coveted 'Blue Riband' in 1909, holding the speed record for twenty years. It was used as a troopship and hospital ship between 1915 – 1918 under the name of 'H.M.S. Tuberose'. The breaking up of the ship commenced on 21st Aug 1935 at Rosyth.   *Ref 3092.*

Ref 3091.

Ship building and launching ceremonies. A regular sight for many years, displaying the success of the shipbuilding industry.

Ref 3093.   *Ref 3094.*

Swan Hunter & Wigham Richardson Ltd.
Neptune Engine Works. (1903 - 1963).
Overhead view of Tyne ship building
at the height of production.
Ref 3095/S2764.

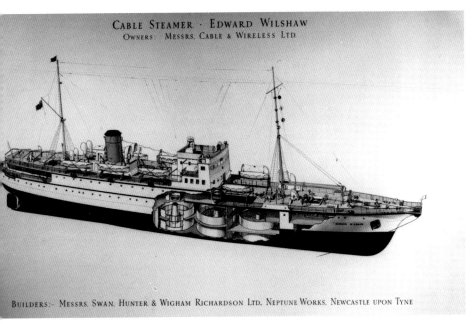

CABLE STEAMER · EDWARD WILSHAW
OWNERS: MESSRS. CABLE & WIRELESS LTD.

BUILDERS:- MESSRS. SWAN, HUNTER & WIGHAM RICHARDSON LTD. NEPTUNE WORKS, NEWCASTLE UPON TYNE

In 1949 Swan Hunter and Wigham Richardson built the largest cable repair ship, the C.S. EDWARD WILSHAW for Cable & Wireless Communications. Named after the company's chairman Sir Edward Wilshaw who became company president in 1947. It was completed at a reported cost of £300,000 with a cable capacity of 18,850 square feet. The ship was based in Mombasa in 1950's, in Gibraltar 1965 – 1970 and in Australia 1970 – 1979. The ship was scrapped in 1979. *Ref 3096.*

Sunderland developed as a coal port but it was Sunderland's place as the largest shipbuilding town in the world that gave the town the fame. The first recorded shipbuilder was Thomas Melville at Hendon in 1346. By 1790 Sunderland was building around nineteen ships per year. It became the most important shipbuilding centre in the country in the 1830's and by 1840 there were 65 shipyards. Over 150 wooden ships were built at Sunderland in 1850 when 2,025 shipwrights worked in the town, with a further 2,000 in related industries. Sunderland's first iron ships were built from 1852 and wooden shipbuilding ceased in 1876. *Ref 3097.*

Ref 3099.

Ref 3098.

COAL MINING in the NORTH EAST.

Robert William Brandling B.A.

Born at Gosforth	6th January	1775.
Died at Brussels	30th December	1848.
Buried at Gosforth	11th January	1849.

The Gosforth Park estate of 2,000 acres was owned from 1509 by the Brandling family. Gosforth House, now known as Brandling House was built between 1755 and 1765 by Charles Brandling and designed by an architect named James Paine, who also developed the designs for the park and lake. The Brandling's suffered financial problems and sold the estate to Thomas Smith in 1852. The house was sold in 1880 to High Gosforth Park Ltd. to create a racecourse on the estate and is now known as Gosforth Park. Robert William Brandling became a Barrister at Law after graduating from St John's College, University of Cambridge in 1794. He was Justice of the Peace for Northumberland and inherited and further developed the Brandling coal dynasty, started by Thomas Brandling (1512 – 1590), with his brother John Brandling. *Ref 3100.*

Saint Hilda Colliery, South Shields, Wagon Way Coal Depot, 1887. A view of loaded coal delivery carts passing over the weighbridge at Waterloo Vale Landsale depot. Originally called Chapter Colliery when Simon Temple opened the colliery on the 23rd April 1810 in the grounds owned by the Dean and Chapter of Durham. The operating cost became too great for Temple and eventually the colliery was acquired by the Brandling's in 1822. The pit was bottomed out at Bensham seam in July 1825, and by the 1830's the colliery was shipping approx. 50,000 tons of coal per year to London. *Ref 3101.*

Saint Hilda Colliery.
Waterloo Vale Coal Depot, 1887.

Saint Hilda colliery played a very important role in the development of ventilation, lighting and safety in the mines. A disastrous explosion in 1839 which killed 51 miners, led to an inquest being established. The inquest found the disaster had resulted from the use of lighted candles in the mine and recommended that their use should be abolished. Subsequently a 'Committee for the Investigation of Accidents in Mines' was formed in South Shields. *Ref 3102.*

Saint Hilda Colliery. 1901. Jigging Screens were widely used for gravity separation, coal processing and coal selection in the coal mining industry. The world's first manual jigging machine was probably manufactured in 1803 and the fixed sieve jigger appeared in 1840. *Ref 3103.*

Saint Hilda Colliery

1810 Colliery opened.

1886 Head stocks erected.

C19th New surface structures added.

C20th Pit head altered, pump house erected next to the shaft.

1940 Ceased production due to World War II.

1985 Head stocks restored.

1989 Pump house partially renovated.

1990 St Hilda's Head stocks listed.

1993 Maintenance of shaft ceased.

Ref 3104.

Saint Hilda Colliery winding engines, erected in 1886. The head stocks and pump house were restored in 1985/1989 to commemorate the 150th anniversary of the disaster which killed 51 miners and led to the introduction of safety lamps in the mines. These structures were grade II listed in 1990. Maintenance of the St Hilda's shaft ceased with the closure of Westoe Colliery as St Hilda's unused shaft had been used as an up cast shaft and emergency escape route. *Ref 3105.*

Harton Colliery - August 21st 1895.

A meeting of senior executives…
Left to Right.
3 x Colliery workers.
then…
Dr. Murphy. (Sunderland)
Mrs. Marshall Stephenson.
(in white)
Dr. O Callaghan. (London)
Mrs. Langman.
Mr George May. (Manager)
Major Dawson.
Mrs. C.W. Anderson.
Mrs. O.Callaghan. (London)
Mr. A.L. Langman.
Mr. J.L. Langman.
Ref 3106.

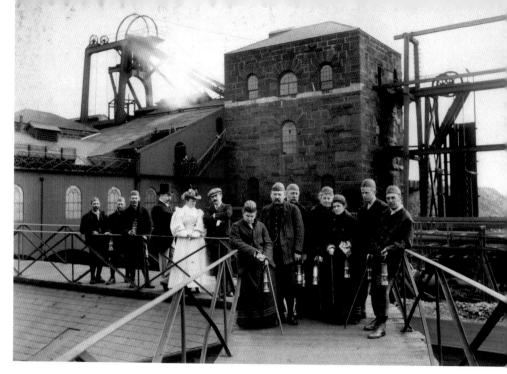

Harton Colliery Coal Depots, 1897,
Harton Coal Company Ltd.was a
South Shields based coal company
formed in 1842 by the Brandling's.
The company operated:-Harton
Colliery, sunk in 1841, Saint Hilda
Colliery, sunk in 1810, Boldon Colliery,
sunk in 1866 and in 1891 absorbed the
Whitburn Coal Company, sunk in 1874.
The Harton Coal Company Ltd.
ceased in 1947 with the
nationalisation of the British
Mining Industry. *Ref 3107.*

Harton Low Staithe River Frontage
1901. When the staithe opened
it was unique in its use of steam
cranes to load waiting ships, being
developed by the Harton Coal Co.
at Mill Dam. Belt conveyor staithes
were first introduced on the Tyne
at the Northumberland Docks
around 1898. *Ref 3108.*

Marsden Railway Station and Limestone Kilns 1901. Marsden & Whitburn Colliery Railway was a twin track line which ran along the North Sea coast from Westoe Lane, South Shields to Whitburn Colliery at Marsden. It had two intermediate stations, Whitburn Colliery (renamed Marsden in 1926) and Marsden which closed in 1926. The railway was built in late 1870's and opened as a private railway in May 1879. The line opened to the public on 19th March 1888 and the passenger service was officially withdrawn on the 14th November 1953. *Ref 3109.*

As well as the colliery and its workers the railway line served the limestone quarries, a paper manufacturer and local farms. After the passenger service was withdrawn, freight trains still continued with most other services closing with Whitburn Colliery on the 8th June 1968. The section Westoe Lane to Westoe Colliery continued open until 1993.

Lighthouse Limestone Quarry, 1901. The quarry began around 1870. One of two quarries at Marsden the other being the Trow Rock Quarry. *Ref 3110.*

Whitburn Colliery, North Side in 1901 also known as Marsden Colliery. It was sunk in 1878 and started production in May 1879. It was served by the Marsden Railway using second hand coaching stock, usually worn out and in poor condition. The trains were very uncomfortable and the coal miners' coaches had wooden seats with all the interior partitions and fittings stripped out. The carriages and service soon gained the nickname 'The Marsden Rattler', which can be seen to the left of the photograph at the miners' station platform. *Ref 3111.*

Park Lane Coal Depot. Gateshead on Tyne. 1887. (owned by Harton Colliery). Brandling Junction Railway Company built a line in the 1830's from Gateshead to South Shields and Monkwearmouth. They also built the railway incline to join Blaydon at Redheugh in order to give access for Newcastle & Carlisle Railway Co. to the coal staithes. This short section opened on the 15th June 1839 with Brandling Junction being Gateshead's first station at Oakwellgate. *Ref 3112.*

The Harton Coal Company was founded in 1842. In 1874 the coal company turned its attention to the vast seam of coal which lay offshore. Problems were soon encountered during the sinking of the shaft at Whitburn, which amounted to immense quantities of water ingress and quicksand. A drift was constructed to enable the water to flow out of the nearby cliffs and into the sea. The company then called in experts from Belgium and by using cast iron tubing and three large pumps were able to solve the flooding problem.

Entrance to Victoria Road Coal and Lime Landsale Depots. South Shields. 1893. *Ref 3113.*

The Harton Coal Company Ltd. General Office (Coal Depots). 1901. *Ref 3114.*

The Keel was an especially built shallow vessel to carry coal, being very long and broad. Coal was carried in the open, without any hatch covers, with side boards being used to hold the heaped coal on deck. The Keel carried eight Newcastle Chaldrons (coal tubs) weighing approx. 21 tons. The crew would utilise the river flows by rowing with the ebb tide to carry coal to the collier and returning empty with the tide. The coal would be unloaded from the Keel by the crew shovelling it or carrying the coal in baskets (as seen in the photo) onto the deck of the collier anchored at the mouth of the river. *Ref 3115.*

Ref 3116.

Ref 3117.

Life Underground in the Mining Industry... for the miners and their ponies.

The first record of ponies replacing child or female labour was in the Durham coalfields in 1750. In 1913 there were approx. 70,000 ponies underground in Britain, normally stabled underground in shaft mines.

Ref 3118.

Ref 3119.

The circus is coming to town. After arriving at the Central Station, Neville Street, Newcastle upon Tyne, the procession of animals would wind its way through the streets of Newcastle to the Town Moor where the Big Top had already been erected. Health and safety was not an important issue which can be seen as a lion is clearly visible behind the people at the front of the coach. *Ref 3120.*

A procession by Judges in regalia through the streets of Newcastle upon Tyne in a ceremony dating from medieval times. Crowds gathered as the dignitaries went to the cathedral where prayers were said for jurors, prisoners and those awaiting trial. *Ref 3121.*

The YMCA (centre building) first moved to Blackett Street, Newcastle upon Tyne, in March 1896. This new building was officially opened on 9th May 1900 by the Duke of Connaught. The building was sold to a London developer in 1964 for $325,000 and leased back to the YMCA at $400 per annum. The magnificent domed building was demolished in 1972 to build Eldon Square shopping centre. The YMCA (Young Men's Christian Association) movement was founded with the purpose of 'the improving of the spiritual condition of young men engaged in the drapery, embroidery and other trades'. *Ref 3122.*

Grey Street, Newcastle upon Tyne was built by Richard Grainger in the 1830's with the help of several architects including John Dobson. It is the home of the Theatre Royal, designed by John and Benjamin Green, which opened in 1837. Grey Street was named after, Northumbrian born, British Prime Minister Earl Grey (1830-1834) whose monument stands at the head of the street. It was voted the 'Best street in the U.K.' by BBC Radio 4 listeners in 2010. *Ref 3123.*

The Newcastle and Gosforth Tramways and Carriage Company was established in 1879, and by 1893 operated 44 trams using 272 horses. These horse drawn trams were replaced with the first electric trams on the 16th December 1901 using overhead cables and running on the old horse tram lines. The advertising on the horse drawn tram reads 'Northumbria's Finest Craster Kippers' and on the horse drawn carriage '23 & 25, Blackett St, Newcastle' – the home of Reid Jewellers, established 1855. *Ref 3124.*

High Bridge, Newcastle upon Tyne, was named after the bridge which crossed the Lort Burn. The burn flowed through the city centre and was used as an open sewer, backing onto the meat market until 1696.
In 1749 the burn was put underground as a continuation of Dean Street. *Ref 3125.*

The Chronicle originated as the Newcastle Chronicle in 1764 as a weekly newspaper, owned by Thomas Stack and his descendants until 1850. It was then acquired by a consortium led by local businessman Mark William Lambert. On the 1st May 1858 the Newcastle Daily Chronicle was launched with Joseph Cowen as its editor, who became its sole owner in 1859. The Chronicle became the most successful newspaper in North East England. It was printed as a broadsheet until the 8th October 1997 when its format was changed to a tabloid sized paper. It is now owned by Trinity Mirror. A crowd with reporters gather outside the Chronicle offices, Newcastle. *Ref 3126.*

In the early 19th century Newcastle's Barge Day, held in May each year on Ascension Day, was a powerful expression of the town's control over the river Tyne.
The Mayor's ceremonial barge led a large flotilla of ships along the Tyne from Newcastle to the mouth of the river. Crowds of people lined the river banks to watch and the festive character of the day was reinforced by rowing races and parties. The Mayor's barge and the Corporation barge, for members of the council, were used on special occasions and utilised a special quay at the back of the old Mansion House in the Close. The system survived till 1974 when the office of Alderman was abolished. *Ref 3127.*

Chollerford Bridge, Northumberland. It is Grade II listed, and situated approx. 4 miles north of Hexham, on the military road, not far from Hadrian's Wall and Chesters Fort. It was constructed in 1775, and was the first stone bridge to be built on the North Tyne after the great floods of 1771 washed away an earlier medieval bridge. *Ref 3128.*

Royal Border Bridge, Railway Viaduct, Berwick upon Tweed, with 28 arches each spanning 60 feet (18m).
It is part of the East Coast Railway line, 121 feet (37m) above the River Tweed. It is Grade 1 listed, was built between 1847 – 1850 and opened by Queen Victoria. Despite its name, the bridge does not in fact span the border between England and Scotland, which is approx. 3 miles further north. *Ref 3129.*

Staward Peel Bridge – The Cupola Bridge – A Grade II listed bridge over the River West Allen, Hayden, Allendale. It was built in 1782 after a proposal of William Johnston and Thomas Forster of Stamfordham. Consisting of 3 arches of unequal segments, the centre one being the larger. It took its name from the type of blast furnace that stood here during the lead mining era.
Built on the site of an earlier bridge built in 1762, which was destroyed in 1765 and another bridge which was lost in the great flood of 1771. *Ref 3130.*

Hexham Bridge built in 1793 – The fourth bridge to be built over the River Tyne at Hexham. The first bridge - Warden Bridge – consisted of two ferries called east and west boats which were replaced in 1770 by a seven arched bridge which was washed away in the great flood of 1771. In 1774 attempts were made for a new bridge which was abandoned due to quicksand. After many difficulties a new bridge, by engineer John Errington, was opened in 1780, but its nine arches were completely overturned in 1782 by a violent hurricane. Eventually famous architect Robert Mylne completed the fourth bridge in 1793 which still stands today. *Ref 3131.*

Miniature Golf Course, Otterburn Hall.

Photograph Philipson Newcastle.

Otterburn Hall – Constructed in 1870 as a country retreat for Lord James Douglas. The land was given to him as recompense for the death of his ancestor Lord James Douglas, who fought at the Battle of Otterburn, and was killed near Otterburn Tower (originally a castle). The tower was founded in 1086, and rebuilt in 1830. The Hall was used during World War II, from 1940 to 1944, as a military hospital. *Ref 3132.*

The ruins of Byland Abbey in Ryedale, North Yorkshire. The Abbey inspired the design of church building throughout the North. It was founded as Savigniac House in 1134, and brought within the Cistercian family in 1147.

The abbey remains include one of the largest cloisters in England. After a rather unsettled start the monks established a thriving monastery, renowned for sheep-rearing and the export of wool. By the late 20th century Byland, Rievaulx and Fountains were described as 'the three shining lights of the North'. *Ref 3133/H2054.*

Ref 3134/G2509.
The Abbey of Rievaulx, near Helmsley, North Yorkshire, was founded in 1132 as the first Cistercian outpost in the North and was the centre for the White Monks to reform and colonise the North of England and Scotland. The Abbey attracted high-profile benefactors such as Henry II (1135 – 1154) and David of Scotland (1124 – 1153). Renowned for its sheep-farming and wool export, it also became an active patron of culture. The Black Death of 1348/49 had a devastating impact on the monastery and by the late 14th century there only remained fourteen monks, three lay-brothers and an abbot. At the Dissolution of the Abbey in 1538, the community numbered twenty-three.

Part of the ruins of the Priory on the Holy Island of Lindisfarne. The site of the earliest Christian monastery in Anglo-Saxon Northumbria. Irish monks, from Iona, settled here in AD 635 by the invitation of the King of Northumbria, Oswald, establishing a monastery and celebrating its Bishop, Cuthbert, who died on the 20th March 687. In 793 the community moved inland due to the first attack in Western Europe by Viking Raiders. Durham monks returned briefly to Lindisfarne in 1069 – 70 and later a new priory was built, linked to Durham's Norman Cathedral, where Cuthbert's relics had come to rest. *Ref 3135.*

Flass Vale, a natural refuge for plants and animals affording an open south east view of Durham Cathedral and Durham Castle.

The Cathedral Church of Christ, Blessed Mary the Virgin and St. Cuthbert of Durham (usually known as Durham Cathedral), the seat of the Anglican Bishop of Durham.

The Bishopric dates from 995, with the present cathedral being founded in AD1093, and regarded as one of the finest examples of Norman Architecture. Designated a UNESCO World Heritage Site along with nearby Durham Castle which faces the Cathedral across Palace Green. The present cathedral replaced the 10th century 'White Church' built as part of a monastic foundation to house the shrine of Saint Cuthbert of Lindisfarne. *Ref 3136.*

The Land of the Prince Bishops. The treasures of Durham Cathedral include relics of St. Cuthbert, the head of St. Oswald of Northumbria and the remains of the Venerable Bede. In addition, it's Dean and Chapter Library contains one of the most complete sets of early printed books in England, the pre - Dissolution monastic accounts and three copies of the Magna Carta. Durham Cathedral and Castle occupy a strategic position on a promontory high above the River Wear and from 1080 the bishopric enjoyed the powers of a bishop Palatine, having military as well as religious leadership and power. Durham Castle was built to the orders of William the Conqueror in 1072 and used as the residence for the Bishop of Durham. The seat of the Bishop of Durham is the fourth most significant in the Church of England hierarchy, and the Bishop stands at the right hand of the monarch at coronations. *Ref 3137.*

Ref 3138. Marsden Grotto, South Shields around 1915 with the Ballroom. The Grotto began its existence in 1782 as a cave and was lived in by 'Jack the Blaster' and his wife. Jack blasted his way to make it a home and when people began visiting down the stairs and path he built, he began to sell food and drink to them. Peter Allon became second resident and in 1828 he enlarged the cave and was granted a licence to sell liquor. Enlargement took several years eventually creating a cave of two storey's in height, including a kitchen and ballroom (see below). *Ref 3139.*

Ref 3140 - Seaburn – the seaside resort of Sunderland and a favourite place of painter L.S.Lowry who took several lengthy holidays here while drawing coastal and industrial scenes. Many of Lowry's paintings can be seen in the Sunderland Museum and Winter Gardens.

The Turner family (Keith Turner and sons) were the operators and managers of the original fairground at Seaburn. Keith Turner's father, Walker Turner, was responsible for the building of the big dipper, which opened in 1955. The nine generation Turner family business operated many fairgrounds including the Spanish City fun park at Whitley Bay from 1994 until its closure in the early 2000's. John Crow and sons operated the Seaburn amusement park from 1988 until its closure in April 2000. *Ref 3141.*

Seaburn also had the Ocean Park Railroad which opened around 1950 and was operated by the local authority. Originally the 15 inch gauge railroad ran inland from the coast road to Dykelands Road with two stations on a ½ mile track. It was later reduced to one station and a ¼ mile track in the form of a U-shape, including a bridge (see photo) over a small, usually dry, stream. The trains operated a push-pull service and was in operation till around 1980. *Ref 3142.*

Tynemouth dates back to the Iron Age as its position in the headland would serve as an excellent defensive position. For centuries its traditions continued with several nations building forts and later castles. Whilst an area of military importance Tynemouth has a long historical association with religion with the first monastery being built there in the 7th century. After the Reformation when Henry VIII took control, the area reverted to a coastal defence being utilised against Napoleon and in both world wars. The jewel in Tynemouth – the Longsands Beach – is a stunningly beautiful expanse, 1200 yards long, lying between the former Tynemouth Swimming Pool and Cullercoats to the north. Longsands has been voted one of the best beaches in the U.K. and Europe. *Ref 3143.*

Bathing machines 'modesty hoods' at Longsands in the 1890's allowing bathing to be enjoyed in private by changing out of their usual clothes, then wading into the sea. Part of the etiquette for sea bathing was rigorously enforced upon women who wished to be 'proper' and not viewed by the opposite sex in their bathing suit. The most common machines had large wheels and were propelled in and out of the sea by horses. Legal segregation of bathing areas ended in 1901. The Plaza, originally known as Tynemouth Palace – Winter Gardens and Aquarium when it opened in 1878. The Plaza was renamed in 1926, but never fulfilled its creator's intention to be the Palace of the North. Schemes have included the Palace Theatre in the 1920's, the Galaland Ballroom in 1933, Night club and restaurant with roller – skating in 1970. It was destroyed by fire on the 10th February 1996. *Ref 3144.*

In 1871 Bank Holidays were created allowing families to escape to the coast, and in 1938 a law was introduced ensuring all workers were entitled to a paid holiday. Nobody went to sunbathe, this was not fashionable and in Victorian times people went to the beach fully clothed. Children loved to play and paddling was so much fun – with their heads fully covered.

Ref 3145.   *Ref 3146.*

In the early 12th century, Whitley was a tiny hamlet owned by the Priory of Tynemouth. The name may be attributed to the de Whitley family, local landowners who had a manor house in the area until 1538. In 1539 the Crown granted possession of the village to the Percy family (the Dukes of Northumberland) who remained major landlords up to the 1950's, hence street names Duke, Duchess, Alnwick, Hotspur etc. The 'Bay' was added to Whitley in 1902 after considerable confusion with Whitby. By 1674, following the dissolution of the Monasteries, the Priory lands and estate were enclosed and divided up, except for the Whitley Links which still remain as open land. *Ref 3147.*

The dome of the Spanish City and Whitley Bay Pleasure Gardens in the distance, which opened on 7th May 1910 as a concert hall, restaurant, roof garden and tearoom. An Empress ballroom was added in 1920 and later the area with its distinctive dome, believed to have been the second largest unsupported concrete dome after St. Paul's Cathedral in the U.K. and now a Grade II listed building, became the renowned funfair.

The area was named 'Spanish City' in 1904 when Charles Elderton, operator of Hebburn Theatre Royal, brought his Toreadors concert party to perform there. 'Spanish City' was immortalised by Dire Straits in their 1980 hit single 'Tunnel of Love' which was played every morning when the park was opened. It was closed to the public in 2000 and the funfair demolished in 2001, and is now awaiting re development. *Ref 3148.*

St. Mary's Lighthouse on the tiny St. Mary's island (also known as Bait Island), just north of Whitley Bay. This small rocky island linked to the mainland by a short causeway built in 1929 and rebuilt in 1965/66, which is submerged at high tide. Prior to the causeway access to the island was by stepping stones. The lighthouse, standing 120 feet (36.6 m) and the adjacent keeper's cottages were built between autumn 1896 and completed in 1898 by John Livingstone Miller of Tynemouth, being illuminated for the first time on 31st August 1898. The lighthouse was built on the site of a monastery / medieval chapel where a small sanctuary light, named St. Katherine's light, acted as a guide to passing ships. The sanctuary light was wrongly ascribed to St. Mary, hence the present name. When operational the lighthouse was run by Trinity House, and was decommissioned in 1984. *Ref 3149.*

Local Traders – Local Service...

R.H.Patterson, Newcastle upon Tyne car retailers, was set up in 1911 to make mining equipment. History relates R.H.Patterson to building the crane which put together the two halves of the city's iconic Tyne Bridge. The crane was then exported to Australia to help build the Sydney Harbour Bridge.

In 1926 Patterson's caught the eye of FORD who were looking for franchises around Britain, and became one of the largest Ford dealers in the North East of England. *Ref 3150.*

Established in 1907, Ringtons family business started when Samuel Smith moved from Leeds and began selling tea from a horse & carriage to the households of Heaton in Newcastle upon Tyne. Samuel Smith began with an initial investment of £250 from business partner William Titterington - the name Ringtons being from the latter part of Titte**rington** and the 'S' from Smith – buying his partner's investment in 1914 when his son Douglas Smith joined the company as a tea delivery boy.

Although two motorised vehicles were introduced in the 1920's the traditional horse & carriage continued delivering door to door until the 1960's. *Ref 3151.*

At one time it seemed everyone shopped at the Co-operative. Doorstep deliveries of milk were made from its dairy, first from a fleet of horse drawn wagons and later by milk float, seen here around 1950. Milk delivery was perfectly suited to these electric vehicles which resulted in 1000's of the floats being utilised after the war. The first battery powered vehicle was built in 1889 by a Mr. Crowther who obtained special permission from Scotland Yard to break the speed limit which was then set at 2 m.p.h. Milkmen filled customer's jugs prior to milk bottles being produced in 1880. *Ref 3152.*

Street vendors, selling goods in the streets from baskets and trays, hand carts and small horse drawn carriages were a common feature of British life. In 1861 it is believed there were 500 watercress sellers and 300 cat meat sellers trading on the streets of London.

Young girls selling matches or young boys selling bootlaces were common place in the 1920's. Girl's selling fruit and vegetables were known as 'costermongers'. *Ref 3153.*

The first newspaper was printed in England in 1641, although earlier news sheets had been produced. The first Newcastle Chronicle, a weekly newspaper, was produced in 1764 with the first edition of the Newcastle Journal being on 12th May 1832 and the Newcastle Daily Chronicle being launched on 1st May 1858. The Paper boy was usually the first paying job available to young teenagers, usually boys. It is believed the first paperboy was in 1833, aged 10 years old. *Ref 3154.*

The ice cream man outside the 'Tyne Bridge Inn'. Ice cream sellers date back to the early 1890's. Small carts were used exclusively by male sellers with the ice cream wrapped in paper or in small bowls.

The Tyne Bridge Inn was owned by Robert Deuchar limited. John Arnison Simson operated one of Newcastle's first breweries, the Sandyford Brewery, which was also acquired by Robert Deuchar. In 1897 Deuchar's expanded into Scotland and in 1941 were acquired by Steel Coulson & Co. of Edinburgh, which was taken over by Newcastle Breweries in 1954. *Ref 3155.*

The 'organ grinder' was a fairly common sight in town streets from the mid Victorian era up to the 1930's. These gentlemen were accompanied by a monkey, sometimes wearing a small red waistcoat and attached to the organ by a chain. The man made his money from coins thrown into his hat or sometimes the monkey carried a small silver cup to collect pennies from passers-by.

The non-musician's organ was played by winding a handle fixed to one end, and the music was coded onto a drum or barrel under the cover.

This photograph is taken around 1890 in Grey Street with Grey's monument and Central Exchange Buildings in view. *Ref 3156.*

The barrel organ was often referred to as a 'hurdy gurdy' in the 18th century. It is a small, portable cranked box instrument with a number of organ pipes, a bellows and a barrel with pins that rotated and played programmed tunes. It was frequently played by poor buskers (street musicians) who entertained the children who danced and listened with excitement and enjoyment while dancing in their bare feet on the rough cobble stoned streets. *Ref 3157.*

Paddy's Market
1890's

Generations of Tyneside poor knew the scene, Paddy's Market on the Quayside, Newcastle upon Tyne where cast off clothes, shoes, boots, ties, ribbons and bows went on sale every week. The sale of second hand clothing had existed for years but tradition suggests Paddy's market started in the early Victorian years by Irish people brought over to break a miners strike and then abandoned. Paddy's Market became a source to survive and provide an income. *Ref 3158.*

The Quayside is one of the oldest parts of Newcastle upon Tyne. The earliest record of there being a market on the quayside is 1717 when a milk market was held there. There were daily markets selling fish, herbs, bread, cloth, leather etc. and on Saturdays and Sundays clothing could be bought. *Ref 3159.*

'It looks like Paddy's Market in here!' – a regularly used phrase especially by your mother. This is the market to which she refers.

There were no regular pitches or licences for 'Paddy's Market', it was a place for the sale of second hand clothes mainly and continued well until the modern 1970's. *Ref 3160.*

Ref 3161. Until the Quayside was refurbished in the late 20th century there was a clothes market held there every Saturday. Prior to the clothes market the area was one of the region's main milk and open meat market. *Ref 3162.*

The wives and daughters of the Northumberland fishermen searched for the bait, digging sand-worms, gathering mussels and seeking limpets and dog crabs. They would bait the hooks and carry a 'creel' of fish weighing up to four stone, on their shoulders. Many taking the journey to Newcastle in order to get a better price for the fish. Also known as the 'fishlass' they would haul and clean the fish, mend nets and stand at the water's edge waiting the return of the fisher men. They would also be there to help launch the lifeboat when needed, wading waist-high into the wild, ice cold sea. *Ref 3163.*

Beach foraging for tasty seafood from the seashore – a pot of clams, a pail of winkles, a haul of mussels, cockles, whelks, and a bag of seaweed from a clean shore to eat for supper. The gatherers needed to be suitably dressed with stout boots for their feet, good woollen garments which fit close to protect against the unkind winds as you were sure to get wet when you were stooping and 'pottering' around. After carrying the seafood home in a bucket or pail containing a little sea water to keep them fresh, they would be placed in cold water mixed with flour to enable the shell fish to 'cleanse' the gut before cooking.
Ref 3164.

Aw's a Cullercoats fish-lass, se cozy an' free
Browt up in a cottage close on by the sea;
An' aw sell fine fresh fish ti poor an' ti rich--
Will ye buy, will ye buy, will ye buy maw fresh fish?

Byeth barefoot and barelegged aw trudge mony a week,
Wi' a creel on mee back an' a bloom on mee cheek;
Aw'll supply ye wi' flat fish, fine skyet, or fresh ling,
And sometimes pennywilks, crabs, an' lobsters aw bring.

Aw work hard for mee livin', frev a frind aw ne'er begs,
An' aw huff the young gents when they peep at my legs;
Aw's hilthy an' hansom, quite willin' and strong,
To toil for my livin', cryin' fish the day long.

'The Cullercoats Fish Lass'
by Edward Corvan 1862

Ref 3165. A group of fishwives sorting herring into baskets, North Shields in 1898. They are wearing their traditional clothes which included a jacket or bed gown, a shawl, an ankle or mid-calf length skirt with a tucked hemline and an apron. *Ref 3166.*

Children at Play ...
at the beach.

Childhood innocence... buckets, spades and sandcastles. Circa. 1900.

People first visited the seaside to improve their health but soon discovered that swimming and playing could be fun as well. With buckets and spades children dig holes, build sand-castles and collect interesting stones and seaweed. *Ref 3167.*

*'Play on the seashore
And gather up shells,
Kneel in the damp sands
Digging wells,*

*Run on the rocks
Where the seaweed slips,
Watch the waves
And the beautiful ships.'*

Shore By **Mary Britton Miller (1883-1979)**

A girl in her bonnet and a smile tells all. *Ref 3168.*

Collecting a pail of water. *Ref 3169.*

Ref 3170. A Victorian Tradition… A paddle in the sea. Simple 'old-fashioned' fun! Donkeys, roundabouts, Punch and Judy, boat trips, beach entertainers, starfish and rock-pools. Tasty informal seaside food – fish and chips, ice cream, candy floss, cockles and whelks and the simple tranquillity of the sea. The local boys enjoy their steeplechase. *Ref 3171.*

Children at Play...
in the street.

Circa. 1900.

The playground game of jacks or chucks, played usually with five small objects. Originally played with sheep bones and known as 'knucklebones', the five objects are thrown up and caught in various ways. The winner is the first player to complete a series of throws. The simplest variation is tossing up a stone, the jack and picking up one or more from the ground while the jack is in the air. *Ref 3172.*

A game of marbles, a popular children's game for centuries. Originally the 'balls' were made of clay or stone until the late 19th century when glass marbles were introduced. There are many variations of the game with a popular one being 'ring tour' played by making a circle on the ground (using chalk, string or drawn in the dirt). The largest marble, called a shooter, was held out, while the other marbles were placed inside the circle. Children crouched down around the circle and took turns flicking the shooter into the circle. Any marbles knocked out by the shooter were kept by the child and the child with the most marbles won the game. *Ref 3173.*

Ref 3174.

Poorer children usually played with home-made toys - a clothes peg turned into a doll, a lump of wood as a toy boat, a piece of rope used for skipping or a swing and rags stuffed with sawdust became a ball or an animal to cuddle. Boys loved to have a 'barra' (wheel barrow), the bigger the better.

Ref 3175.

Ref 3176.

Ref 3177. Newcastle cattle and sheep market was first held on 27th June 1830 on a small patch of land, as the nearest market was held in Morpeth. Around 1842 a larger area bounded by Scotswood Road, Westmorland Road and Marlborough Crescent was adopted with a Keeper's House built at the same time and attributed to John Dobson. Later in 1870 the adjacent 'Knox's Field', which held the 'Hoppings', was added and covered with cattle pens. After the market the livestock were led through the streets to the slaughter houses nearby.

Children were encouraged to play games for light exercise. A game of 'hoop and stick', also known by many other names, was very common and played by children beating a large wooden hoop, or iron wheel, with a stick, forcing it to roll like a wheel. The object was to keep the hoop moving. Simple games like 'kick the can' and 'hide the can' kept children entertained for hours. *Ref 3178.*

Ref 3179. Most games for girls did not involve physical activity as they were taught skills needed to care for the household. Children were not allowed to play card games because parents feared such activities would lead to gambling. Special children's card games, such as 'Old Maid' were created to overcome this fear, but many children just played in the street with their friends and pets, scruffy, mucky and barefoot.

Ref 3180. Parents were never concerned about danger! Children would go off for the day with their paste or jam sandwiches. On the way home they could stop and cut each other's hair (see the cuttings on the ground) then have a wash in the outside cold water tap and go home for tea. Mam was always happy to see her children return clean and they didn't have to get washed again in the 'mucky' bath water that Dad and others had left in the tin bath or wash tub.

During the 1800's and early 1900's children of the poor were expected to help towards the family budget, often working long hours in dangerous jobs for low wages. Agile boys were employed by the chimney sweep, small children were employed to scramble under machinery to retrieve cotton bobbins and children worked in coal mines, crawling through tunnels too narrow and low for adults. Children worked as errand boys, crossing sweepers, shoe blacks, or sold matches, flowers and other cheap goods. But these wonderful images of children capture the true meaning of childhood. They are a joy to find and a privilege to share them with you. We hope you enjoy every one. *Ref 3181.*

Children loved leapfrog. One or more would bend over and clutch their knees while others would run and put their hands on their backs and jump over. Usually a clout on the head when they missed! *Ref 3182.*

Ref 3183.

'I wonder what images we will find next?'